Nomads on a Barren Plain:
Poems on Life and Loss

by

Michelle Spaw

Finishing Line Press
Georgetown, Kentucky

Nomads on a Barren Plain:
Poems on Life and Loss

Copyright © 2021 by Michelle Spaw
ISBN 978-1-64662-457-7 First Edition
All rights reserved under International and Pan-American Copyright Conventions. No part of this book may be reproduced in any manner whatsoever without written permission from the publisher, except in the case of brief quotations embodied in critical articles and reviews.

ACKNOWLEDGMENTS

A sincere thank you to the entire team at Finishing Line Press, in particular Leah Maines, Kevin Maines, Christen Kincaid, and Mimi David. Your help and support in making this book a reality has been an incredible experience. I am also appreciative to all those who shared their personal accounts of loss with me. (You know who you are.) At some point in life, grief is a story we all tell. From you, I learned many lessons, for which I will be forever grateful.

Publisher: Leah Huete de Maines
Editor: Christen Kincaid
Cover Art: Kathryn Michelle Spaw
Author Photo: Kathryn Michelle Spaw
Cover Design: Elizabeth Maines McCleavy

Printed in the USA on acid-free paper.
Order online: www.finishinglinepress.com
also available on amazon.com

Author inquiries and mail orders:
Finishing Line Press
P. O. Box 1626
Georgetown, Kentucky 40324
U. S. A.

Table of Contents

Phoenix 1

Pompeii 2

Fade to Black 3

Trespass 4

History 5

The Mariner's Widow (La Herradura, 1562) 6

The Last Prayer 7

Deathbed 8

Forgiveness 9

Forget-me-not (Poem for April 1st) 10

Ghost Ship 11

Walkabout 12

Shape-shift 13

Sentence 14

Funeral 15

Tending Grief 16

Untethered 17

Pluck 18

Just Look 19

Reunion 20

Transition 21

Hourglass 22

Epilogue 23

For Jim

Phoenix

She's the ashes
of a Viking ship,
set on fire
long ago,
and the embers
of a peasant girl
burning at the stake;
she's every flame
of every candle,
a bonfire in the sky.

Pompeii

I remember
warm summer days,
days of pomegranates
and figs.
Before we were
covered in dust,
before we
said farewell,
before our city
became our tomb,
I looked at you
one last time,
your eyes
blue as lapis.

Fade to Black

Darkness is
a shaman's cave,
a sacred blindfold,
leading you
to a deep, deep well
where you
are baptized
by your sorrow.

Trespass

She looks
at her wrists
and sees a map,
a pilgrimage
to a promised land.
Along this road
she'll leave her sins,
and wait for mercy
as she heads north.

History

I wonder
who will
find them,
the memories
you left behind.
Maybe in
a thousand years
they will
be discovered
by children
playing in a field
or unearthed
by scholars
tracing lost worlds.

The Mariner's Widow
     (La Herradura, 1562)

It was under
an autumn moon,
sailing from
the coast of Spain
that I stood sentry
beneath the mast
as ghosts
went swimming
in the sea.
I tucked a rose
into my hair,
and for them
I played
my castanets.

The Last Prayer

Like the fossil
of a small bird
forever embracing
the earth,
we fold
our wings inward,
a final repose,
and wait
for our deliverance.

Deathbed

I can tell
she is
afraid to go.
If only she knew
that all this time,
all her life,
she'd already
been sitting
among lions.

Forgiveness

I took
the lightning
as a talisman,
before it could
strike again,
and only then
did I find
my truth:
the rock
that broke me
had concealed
a sword.

Forget-me-not
(Poem for April 1st)

This is how
I'll remember
that day:
as a delicate corsage,
pressed between pages
of a favorite book,
the hero
never to return,
a woman
now alone.

Ghost Ship

They sit in taverns
and raise a glass.
They try to understand.
Strangers are told
she went down
in a storm,
that sirens drew her
to the ocean floor.
But really,
she decided
to just disappear,
but might
sail again
one day.

Walkabout

I'm going
to carve symbols
into the sky,
like hieroglyphs
in a pharaoh's tomb;
lines engraved
on every star,
a language
full of stones.

Shape-shift

I know
about spirits
who bleach away
in the sun.
A coyote skull
whose teeth
still bite:
the stuff
of nightmares
and bedclothes torn,
and invisible ruins.

Sentence

Your words
wrapped me
like a hangman's rope,
a black-fringed tendril
dipped in the past.
How softly you spoke,
how softly I'll hang
from
that
velvet
gallows.

Funeral

She is
surrounded
by a field
of white:
the white
of a farmhouse,
the white
of nearly
a hundred Decembers,
the white
of lilies
laid against marble,
the white
of a chariot,
going home.

Tending Grief

We are nomads
on a barren plain,
pulling seeds
from vacant soil,
and butterflies
in an empty garden,
sipping nectar
no one else can see.

Untethered

I don't mind
being set adrift;
from
discarded splinters
I built
a raft.

Pluck

You were
the flower
that bloomed late,
long into November,
and I was
the girl
who found you,
my pockets
full of rain.

Just Look

Out of nothing,
often comes treasure:
a monk's bowl
filling with rice,
the hollow
of a
mockingbird tree.

Reunion

When the end
finally comes,
we should shut the door,
and let the ghosts
tell their stories.
They have waited
a long time
for this day,
to talk again
about when
they were young,
and sat on porch swings,
and drew lanterns close
during storms.

Transition

Sometimes I pretend
my soul is a mountain,
covered in prayer flags
touching the sky.
Sometimes I pretend
the moon is a wizard,
turning tides into songs
that put me to sleep.
And sometimes I pretend
that I'm finally crossing over,
now that I've pawned
the last of my gold.

Hourglass

Someday,
leaves will
cover my bed,
and
I'll thank them
for the
handmade quilt.

Epilogue

Next time:
It won't be
a silver band
or sonnets
from a balcony.
It will be
a sudden glance,
the one
that makes
me blush.

Michelle Spaw, mixed-media artist and writer, has worked in numerous creative fields. Since the 1980's, her focus has been the visual language of painting, which later evolved into the practice of storytelling through poetry, where she explores subjects of love and loss, death and grief, and the journey of the soul. She lives in Kansas City, Missouri.

www.ingramcontent.com/pod-product-compliance
Lightning Source LLC
LaVergne TN
LVHW041519070426
835507LV00012B/1693